Contemporary Coffeehouse
SONGS

M000092555

ISBN 978-1-4584-3789-1

HAL•LEONARD®
CORPORATION

7777 W. BLUEMOUND RD. P.O. BOX 13819 MILWAUKEE, WI 53213

Visit Hal Leonard Online at
www.halleonard.com

Contents

BABYLON

Words and Music by
DAVID GRAY

Moderately fast

Fri-day night, _ I'm go-ing no - where;

all the lights _ are chang-ing green ____ to red. ____

BANANA PANCAKES

Words and Music by
JACK JOHNSON

BURN ONE DOWN

Words and Music by
BEN HARPER

Moderately

Let us __ burn one from end to end, and pass it o-ver to me, __

* *Guitarists: Tune down one whole step (low to high): D-G-C-F-A-D.*

My choice __ is what I choose to do. And if it's caus - in' no harm, __ it should-n't

Herb, the __ gift from the earth, and what's from the earth __ is of the

both - er you. __ Your choice __ is who you choose to be. And if you're

great - est worth. __ So be - fore you __ knock it, try it first. Oh, you'll

CODA

Em   D   C
Dm   C   Bb

I'm gon-na burn ___ one... _____ Oh.

G
F

G
F

Repeat and Fade

BLACK HORSE
AND THE CHERRY TREE

Words and Music by
KATIE TUNSTALL

Moderately, with a beat

Woo, hoo, _____ woo, hoo, woo,

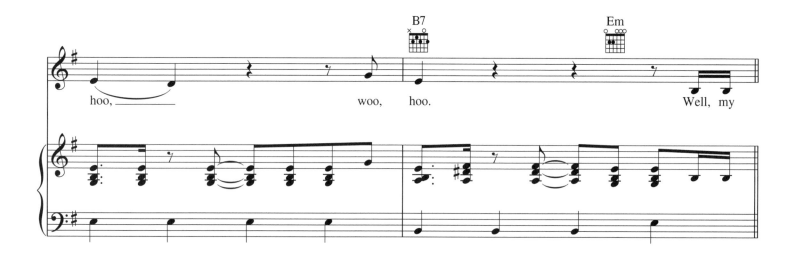

hoo, _____ woo, hoo. Well, my

heart knows me bet-ter than I know my-self ___ so I'm ___ gon-na let it do all the talk-in'. Woo,

CHASING CARS

Words and Music by GARY LIGHTBODY,
TOM SIMPSON, PAUL WILSON,
JONATHAN QUINN and NATHAN CONNOLLY

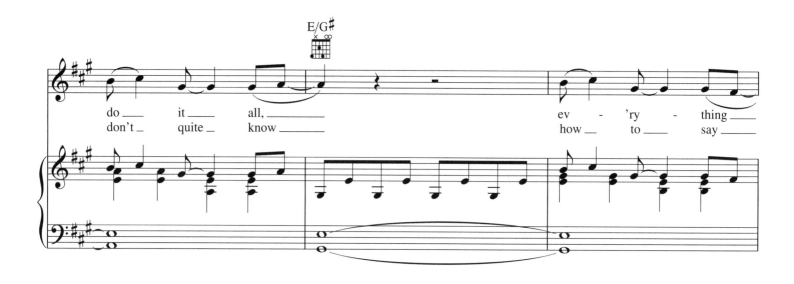

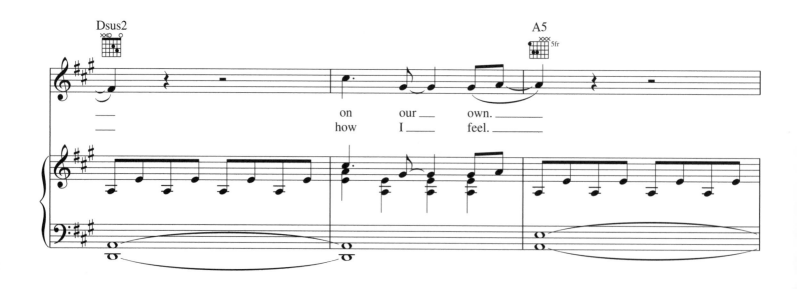

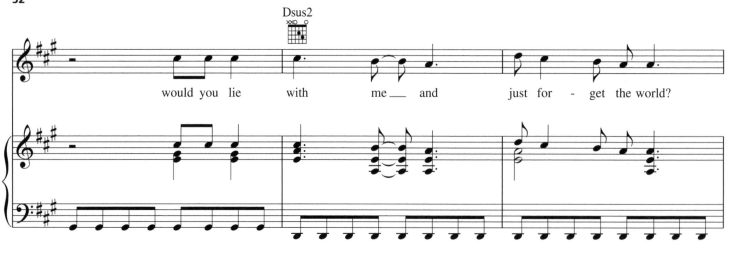

would you lie with me __ and just for - get the world?

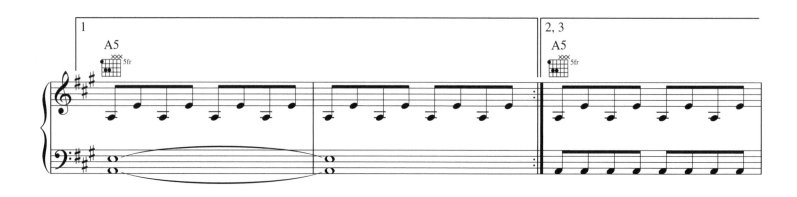

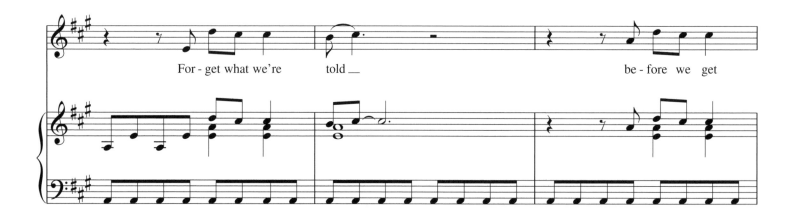

For - get what we're told __ be - fore we get

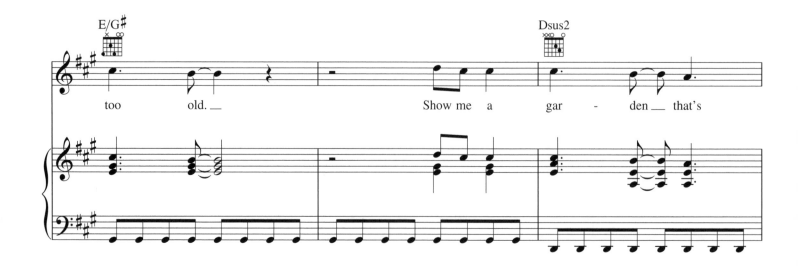

too old. __ Show me a gar - den __ that's

FALLIN' FOR YOU

Words and Music by COLBIE CAILLAT
and RICK NOWELS

COME ON GET HIGHER

Words and Music by MATT NATHANSON
and MARK WEINBERG

COME PICK ME UP

Words and Music by RYAN ADAMS
and VAN ALSTON

When they call ___ your name, ___ will you walk ___ right up

CONSTANT CRAVING

Words and Music by k.d. lang
and BEN MINK

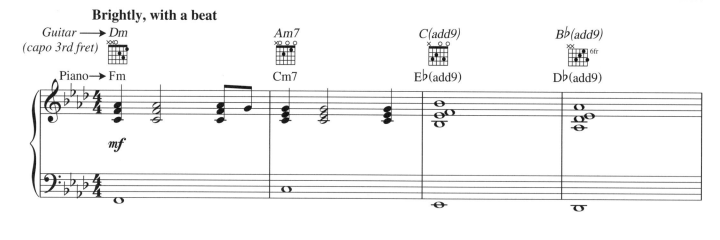

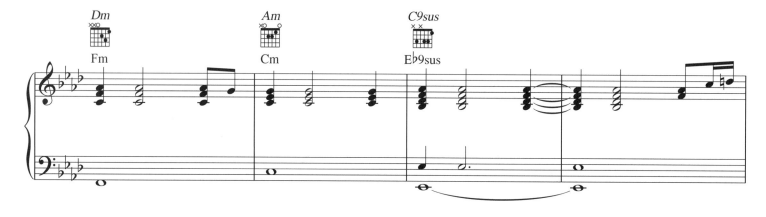

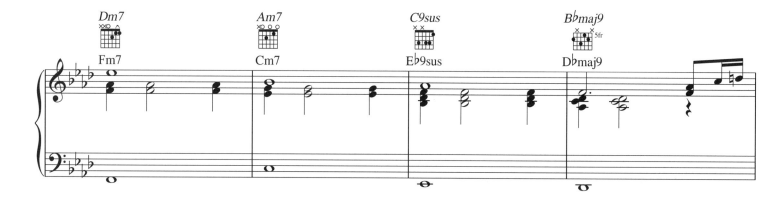

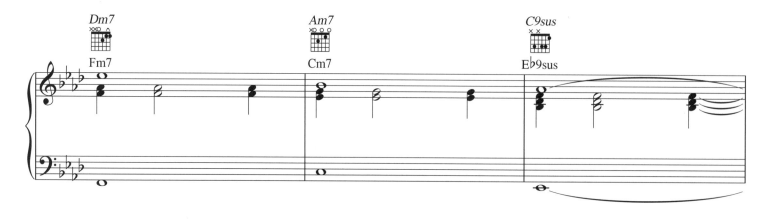

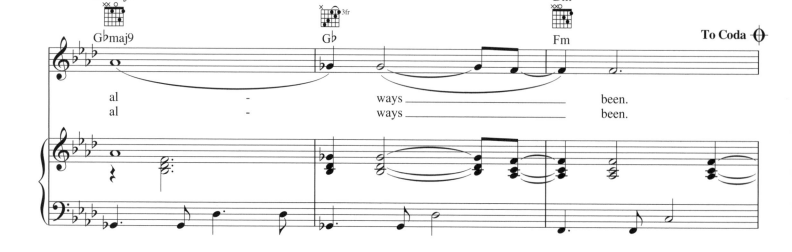

58

DON'T KNOW WHY

Words and Music by
JESSE HARRIS

ELDERLY WOMAN BEHIND THE COUNTER IN A SMALL TOWN

Words and Music by STONE GOSSARD,
JEFFREY AMENT, EDDIE VEDDER,
MICHAEL McCREADY and DAVID ABBRUZZESE

FUGITIVE

Words and Music by ROBBIE MALONE,
KEITH PRIOR and DAVID GRAY

an - swer "none of the a - bove?" ___ Crouched in a hole like a mud-streaked fu - gi - tive. ___
flesh and blood and cam - ou - flage ___ in - to the wall; now ___ some-thing's got - ta give. ___

Am
Gsus
3fr
Got - ta live.
C
C/B♭
If on - ly for a sec - ond,
I see it twin - kling in your eye.
Am
Gsus
3fr
C
Got - ta try.
The world that you're for - sak - ing
C/B♭
Am
is sure - ly more than just a lie.
Got - ta try.

HALF OF MY HEART

Words and Music by
JOHN MAYER

Moderately fast

I was born _____ in the arms _____ of i-mag-i-nar-y _____
I was made _____ to be-lieve _____ I'd nev-er love _____ some-bod-y _____

FAST CAR

Words and Music by
TRACY CHAPMAN

HALLELUJAH

Words and Music by
LEONARD COHEN

Chorus

lu - jah. _____ Hal - le - lu - jah. _____ Hal - le -

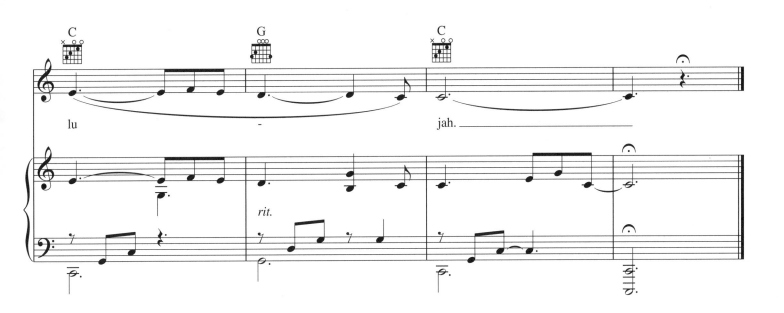

lu - jah. _____

Additional Lyrics

4. There was a time you let me know
   What's real and going on below.
   But now you never show it to me, do you?
   And remember when I moved in you.
   The holy dark was movin', too,
   And every breath we drew was Hallelujah.
   Chorus

5. Maybe there's a God above,
   And all I ever learned from love
   Was how to shoot at someone who outdrew you.
   And it's not a cry you can hear at night.
   It's not somebody who's seen the light.
   It's a cold and it's a broken Hallelujah.
   Chorus

I'D RATHER BE WITH YOU

Words and Music by
JOSHUA RYAN RADIN

*Recorded a half step lower.

104

I WILL FOLLOW YOU INTO THE DARK

Words and Music by
BENJAMIN GIBBARD

ICE CREAM

Words and Music by
SARAH McLACHLAN

Your love is bet-ter than ice_____ cream,
Your love is bet-ter than choc - 'late,

Vocal written one octave higher than sung.

IF IT MAKES YOU HAPPY

Words and Music by JEFF TROTT
and SHERYL CROW

sad?

THE LAZY SONG

Words and Music by BRUNO MARS,
ARI LEVINE, PHILIP LAWRENCE
and KEINAN WARSAME

Moderately, in 2

To-day I don't feel like do-ing an - y-thing.

(whistle) _____ I just wan-na lay in my bed. _____

(whistle) _____ Don't feel like pick-ing up _____ my phone, _ so

* Recorded a half step lower.

LEAST COMPLICATED

Words and Music by
EMILY SALIERS

132

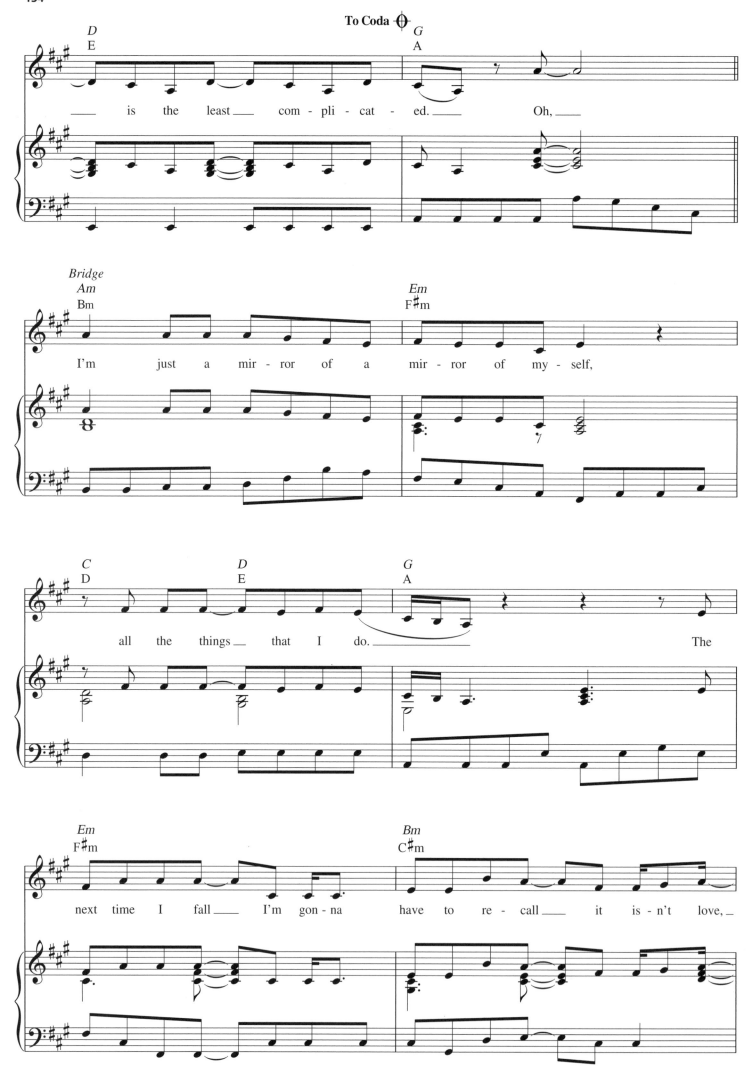

LITTLE LIES

Words and Music by
DAVE BARNES

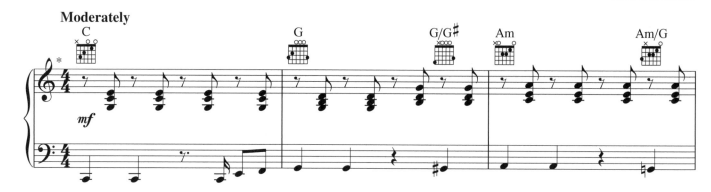

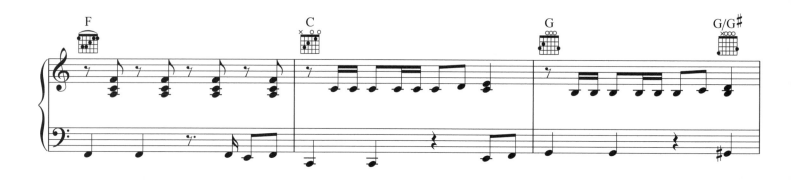

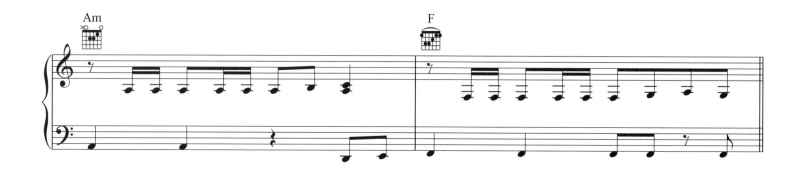

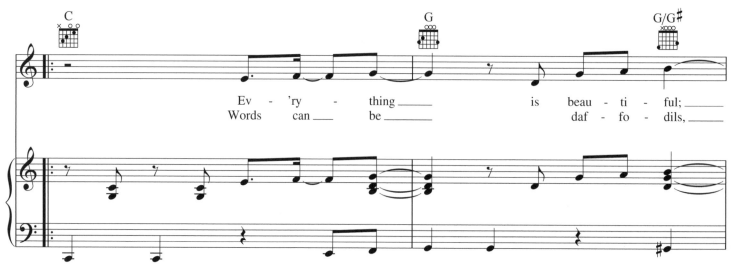

Ev - 'ry - thing _____ is beau - ti - ful; _____
Words can _____ be _____ daf - fo - dils, _____

Recorded a half step higher.

LET HIM FLY

Words and Music by
PATTY GRIFFIN

Lucky

Words and Music by JASON MRAZ,
COLBIE CAILLAT and TIMOTHY FAGAN

Moderately bright

Do you hear me talk-ing to you? A-cross the wa-ter, a-cross the deep blue o-cean, un-der the o-pen sky. Oh, my, ba-by, I'm try-ing.

Boy, I hear you in my

*Female vocal sung one octave lower than written.

*Substitute half rest on D.S.

NAME

Words and Music by
JOHN RZEZNIK

Moderately, not too slow

even though ___ the mo- ment passed ___ me by, ___ I
scars are sou- ve- nirs ___ you nev- er lose, ___ the
I think ___ a- bout ___ you all ___ the time, ___ but

And

And I won't tell 'em your name.

The

MEET VIRGINIA

Words and Music by PAT MONAHAN,
JAMES STAFFORD and ROB HOTCHKISS

166

ONE OF US

Words and Music by
ERIC BAZILIAN

PUT YOUR RECORDS ON

Words and Music by JOHN BECK,
STEVEN CHRISANTHOU and CORINNE BAILEY RAE

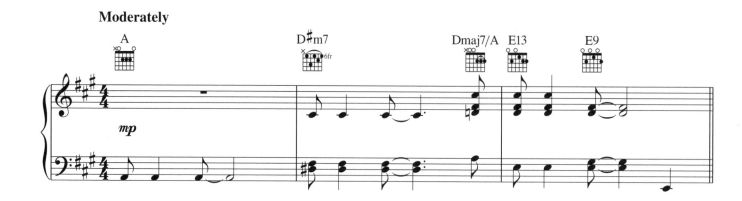

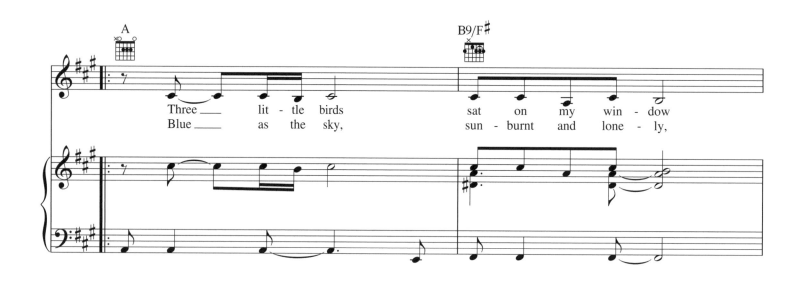

Three ___ lit - tle birds sat on my win - dow
Blue ___ as the sky, sun - burnt and lone - ly,

and they told me I don't need to wor - ry. ___
sip - pin' tea in a bar by the road - side. ___

SAVE TONIGHT

Words and Music by
EAGLE EYE CHERRY

ROUND HERE

Words by ADAM DURITZ
Music by DAVE JANUSKO, DAN JEWETT,
CHRIS ROLDAN and DAVID BRYSON

188

SHE RUNS AWAY

Words and Music by
DUNCAN SHEIK

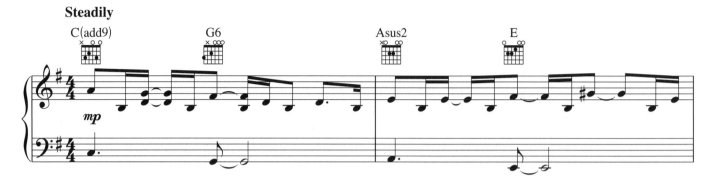

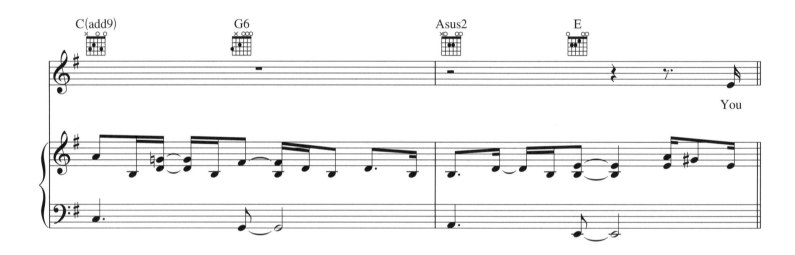

You

may not see the end__ of it,   but luck-i-ly__ she comes a-round.__   It

saw the symp-toms right__ a-way   and spoke to me__ in po-et-ry.__   Some-

(D.S.) ev-'ry-thing__ will turn__ a-round.   She be-comes__ so se-ri-ous.__

She runs a - way.

To Coda

And

THE SCIENTIST

Words and Music by GUY BERRYMAN,
JON BUCKLAND, WILL CHAMPION
and CHRIS MARTIN

I'm go-ing back to the start.

6TH AVENUE HEARTACHE

Words and Music by
JAKOB DYLAN

SONGBIRD

Words and Music by
CHRISTINE McVIE

you, I love you, I love you like nev-er be-fore.

Guitar solo

THE SPACE BETWEEN

Words and Music by DAVID J. MATTHEWS
and GLEN BALLARD

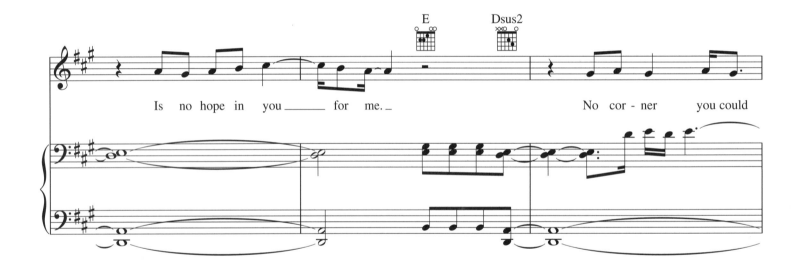

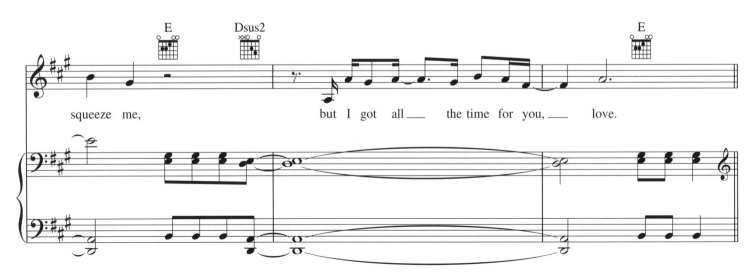

me hid-ing, wait-ing for you. ___ The space be-tween your ___ heart and ___

___ mine _____ is the space ___ we'll fill with time. The space be-tween...

Repeat and Fade

Additional Lyrics

2. The rain that falls splashed in your heart,
   Ran like sadness down the window into your room.

3. The space between our wicked lies is where
   We hope to keep safe from pain.

4. Take my hand 'cause
   We're walking out of here.

5. Oh, right out of here.
   Love is all we need, dear.

SUNNY CAME HOME

Words and Music by SHAWN COLVIN
and JOHN LEVENTHAL

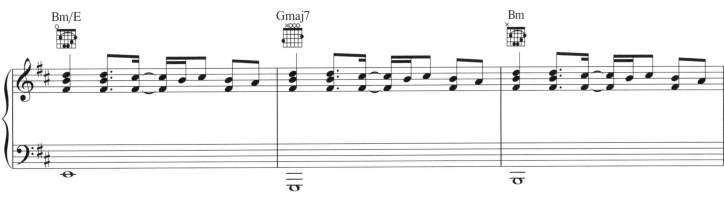

STAY

Words and Music by
LISA LOEB

* Recorded a half step higher.

STEAL MY KISSES

Words and Music by
BEN HARPER

235

al - ways have to steal my kiss - es from you.

STOLEN

Words and Music by
CHRIS CARRABBA

Moderately slow

Lyrics:
We watch the sea-son pull up its own stakes ___ and catch the last week-end ___ of the last week be-fore the gold ___ and the glim-mer have been re-placed. ___ An-oth-er sun-soaked sea-son fades ___ a-way.

THANK YOU

Words and Music by PAUL HERMAN
and DIDO ARMSTRONG

* *Recorded a half step lower.*
** *Vocal written one octave higher than sung.*

Push the door; — I'm home — at — last, — and I'm soak - ing through — and through. —

TOM'S DINER

Music and Lyrics by
SUANNE VEGA

Moderate groove

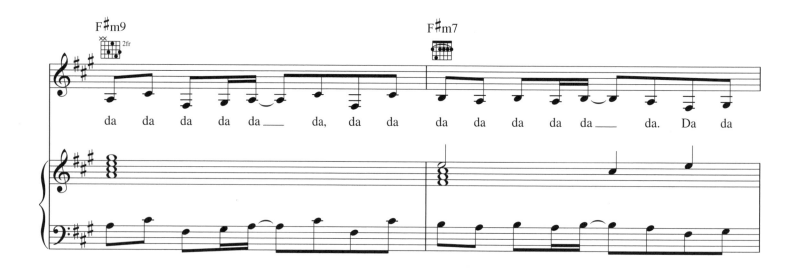

TORN

Words and Music by PHIL THORNALLEY,
SCOTT CUTLER and ANNE PREVIN

Moderate Rock

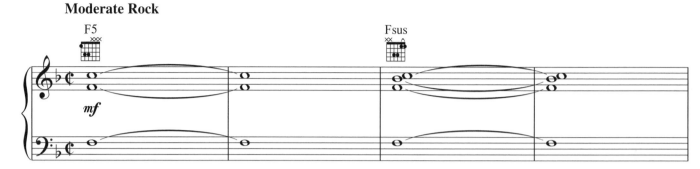

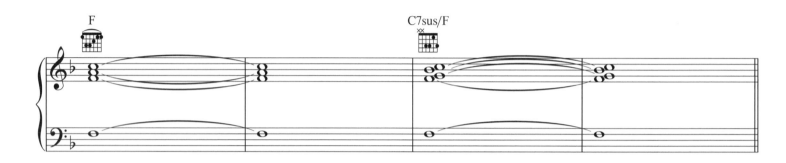

Well, you / I thought I saw a man brought
So, I / I guess the for-tune tell-

to life. / He was warm,
a - dored. / You don't seem to know
-er's right. / I should-'ve seen

THE WAY I AM

Words and Music by
INGRID MICHAELSON

*Chords implied by bass (next 20 bars).

If you ___ were fall - ing, ___ then I ___ would catch you. ___ You need ___ a light, ___ I'd find a match. ___ 'Cause I _____ (I _____

TROUBLE

Words and Music by
RAY LaMONTAGNE

Moderately, in 2

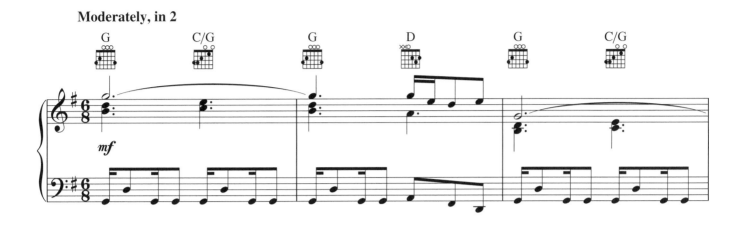

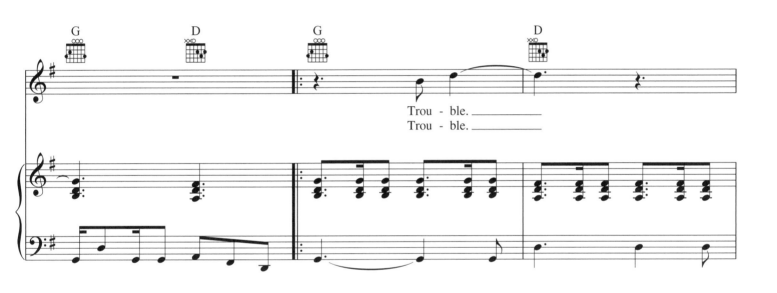

Trou - ble. _____
Trou - ble. _____

Trou - ble, trou - ble, trou - ble, trou - ble.
Trou - ble, trou - ble, trou - ble, trou - ble.

Trou - ble been
Feels like ev - 'ry

WHAT I AM

Words and Music by BRANDON ALY,
EDIE BRICKELL, JOHN BUSH,
JOHN HOUSER and KENNETH WITHROW

285

WHO WILL SAVE YOUR SOUL

Lyrics and Music by
JEWEL KILCHER

* Originally sung an octave lower.

YOU LEARN

Lyrics by ALANIS MORISSETTE
Music by ALANIS MORISSETTE and GLEN BALLARD

WONDERWALL

Words and Music by
NOEL GALLAGHER

Big Books of Music

Our "Big Books" feature big selections of popular titles under one cover, perfect for performing musicians, music aficionados or the serious hobbyist. All books are arranged for piano, voice, and guitar, and feature stay-open binding, so the books lie flat without breaking the spine.

BIG BOOK OF BALLADS – 2ND ED.
62 songs.
00310485 ....$19.95

BIG BOOK OF BIG BAND HITS
84 songs.
00310701 ....$22.99

BIG BOOK OF BLUEGRASS SONGS
70 songs.
00311484 ....$19.95

BIG BOOK OF BLUES
80 songs.
00311843 ....$19.99

BIG BOOK OF BROADWAY
70 songs.
00311658 ....$19.95

BIG BOOK OF CHILDREN'S SONGS
55 songs.
00359261 ....$16.99

GREAT BIG BOOK OF CHILDREN'S SONGS
76 songs.
00310002 ....$14.95

FANTASTIC BIG BOOK OF CHILDREN'S SONGS
66 songs.
00311062 ....$17.95

MIGHTY BIG BOOK OF CHILDREN'S SONGS
65 songs.
00310467 ....$14.95

REALLY BIG BOOK OF CHILDREN'S SONGS
63 songs.
00310372 ....$17.99

BIG BOOK OF CHILDREN'S MOVIE SONGS
66 songs.
00310731 ....$19.99

BIG BOOK OF CHRISTMAS SONGS – 2ND ED.
126 songs.
00311520 ....$19.95

BIG BOOK OF CLASSIC ROCK
77 songs.
00310801 ....$22.95

BIG BOOK OF CLASSICAL MUSIC
100 songs.
00310508 ....$19.99

BIG BOOK OF CONTEMPORARY CHRISTIAN FAVORITES – 3RD ED.
50 songs.
00312067 ....$21.99

BIG BOOK OF COUNTRY MUSIC – 2ND ED.
63 songs.
00310188 ....$19.95

BIG BOOK OF COUNTRY ROCK
64 songs.
00311748 ....$19.99

BIG BOOK OF EARLY ROCK N' ROLL
99 songs.
00310398 ....$19.95

BIG BOOK OF '50S & '60S SWINGING SONGS
67 songs.
00310982 ....$19.95

BIG BOOK OF FOLK POP ROCK
79 songs.
00311125 ....$24.95

BIG BOOK OF FOLKSONGS
125 songs.
00312549 ....$19.99

BIG BOOK OF FRENCH SONGS
70 songs.
00311154 ....$19.95

BIG BOOK OF GERMAN SONGS
78 songs.
00311816 ....$19.99

BIG BOOK OF GOSPEL SONGS
100 songs.
00310604 ....$19.95

BIG BOOK OF HYMNS
125 hymns.
00310510 ....$17.95

BIG BOOK OF IRISH SONGS
76 songs.
00310981 ....$19.95

BIG BOOK OF ITALIAN FAVORITES
80 songs.
00311185 ....$19.99

BIG BOOK OF JAZZ – 2ND ED.
75 songs.
00311557 ....$19.95

BIG BOOK OF LATIN AMERICAN SONGS
89 songs.
00311562 ....$19.95

BIG BOOK OF LOVE SONGS
80 songs.
00310784 ....$19.95

BIG BOOK OF MOTOWN
84 songs.
00311061 ....$19.95

BIG BOOK OF MOVIE MUSIC
72 songs.
00311582 ....$19.95

BIG BOOK OF NOSTALGIA
158 songs.
00310004 ....$24.99

BIG BOOK OF OLDIES
73 songs.
00310756 ....$19.95

BIG BOOK OF RAGTIME PIANO
63 songs.
00311749 ....$19.95

BIG BOOK OF RHYTHM & BLUES
67 songs.
00310169 ....$19.95

BIG BOOK OF ROCK
78 songs.
00311566 ....$22.95

BIG BOOK OF SOUL
71 songs.
00310771 ....$19.95

BIG BOOK OF STANDARDS
86 songs.
00311667 ....$19.95

BIG BOOK OF SWING
84 songs.
00310359 ....$19.95

BIG BOOK OF TORCH SONGS – 2ND ED.
75 songs.
00310561 ....$19.99

BIG BOOK OF TV THEME SONGS
78 songs.
00310504 ....$19.95

BIG BOOK OF WEDDING MUSIC
77 songs.
00311567 ....$19.95

HAL•LEONARD® CORPORATION
7777 W. BLUEMOUND RD. P.O. BOX 13819 MILWAUKEE, WI 53213

0812